PIANO•VOCAL•GUITAR

Billboard ®

TOP ROCK 'N' ROLL HITS OF THE 60'S

W9-CQU-001

This publication is not for sale in
the EC and/or Australia
or New Zealand.

ISBN 0-7935-0831-2

HAL•LEONARD® CORPORATION
7777 W. BLUEMOUND RD. P.O. BOX 13819 MILWAUKEE, WI 53213

TOP ROCK 'N' ROLL

HITS OF THE 60's

THE BIRDS AND THE BEES

Words and Music by
HERB NEWMAN

Let me tell ya 'bout the birds and the bees and the flow-ers and the trees and the

moon up a-bove and a thing___ called love _____

Let me tell ya 'bout the stars in the sky and a girl and a guy and the

facts of life___ start-ing from "A" to "Z". Let me tell ya 'bout the

birds and the bees and the flow-ers and the trees and the moon up a-bove

and a thing___ called love.___

Let me tell ya 'bout the love.___

BORN TO BE WILD

Moderate Rock

Words and Music by
MARS BONFIRE

make it hap - pen, take the world in a love em - brace._

Fire__ all of your guns__ at once__ and ex - plode__ in - to space.__

— — — Like a true__ na·ture child__ we were born,_

— born to be wild.__ We have climbed so high,___

BREAKING UP IS HARD TO DO

Words and Music by NEIL SEDAKA
and HOWARD GREENFIELD

Lyrics:

You tell me that you're leav-ing, I can't be-lieve it's true,

girl, there's just no liv-ing with-out you.

Don't take your love a - way from me.

DUKE OF EARL

Words and Music by EARL EDWARDS
EUGENE DIXON and BERNICE WILLIAMS

BRISTOL STOMP

Words and Music by KAL MANN
and DAVE APPELL

CALENDAR GIRL

Words and Music by HOWARD GREENFIELD
and NEIL SEDAKA

CAN'T BUY ME LOVE

Words and Music by JOHN LENNON
and PAUL McCARTNEY

MCA music publishing

27

CARA MIA

By JULIO TRAPANI
and LEE LANGE

GIMME SOME LOVIN'

Words and Music by SPENCER DAVIS,
MUFF WINWOOD, and STEVE WINWOOD

Hey!

Well, my tem - p'ra - ture's ris - ing and my
feel so good;___ ev - 'ry -
feel so good;___ ev - 'ry -

GLORIA

Words and Music by
VAN MORRISON

GROOVIN'

Words and Music by FELIX CAVALIERE
and EDWARD BRIGATI, JR.

GOOD LOVIN'

Words and Music by RUDY CLARK
and ART RESNICK

Brightly

One two three! Good love.   Good

love.   Good love.

Good love.

(scat on "doo's")

GOODBYE CRUEL WORLD

Words and Music by
GLORIA SHAYNE

HEY JUDE

Words and Music by JOHN LENNON
and PAUL McCARTNEY

I CAN SEE FOR MILES

Words and Music by
PETER TOWNSHEND

I GOT YOU
(I FEEL GOOD)

Words and Music by
JAMES BROWN

Woh! I feel good. ____

I knew that I would ____ now.
Ah, sug - ar and spice. ____

I feel ____ good.
I feel ____ nice.

THE LION SLEEPS TONIGHT
(WIMOWEH) (MBUBE)

New lyric and revised music by HUGO PERETTII,
LUIGI CREATORE, GEORGE WEISS and ALBERT STANTON
Based on a song by SOLOMON LINDA and PAUL CAMPBELL

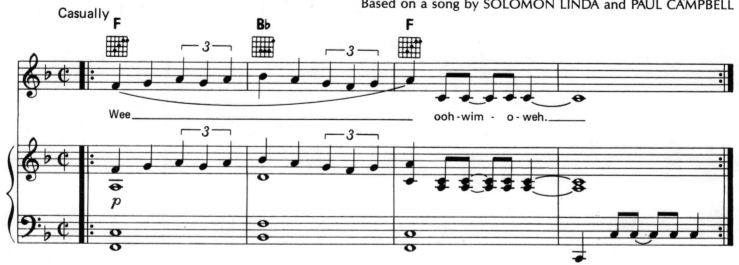

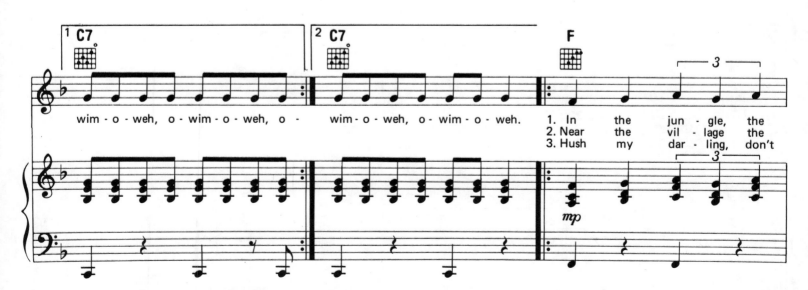

I WANT TO HOLD YOUR HAND

Words and Music by JOHN LENNON
and PAUL McCARTNEY

70

I'M A MAN

Words and Music by STEVE WINWOOD
and JIMMY MILLER

74

I'VE GOTTA GET A MESSAGE TO YOU

Words and Music by BARRY GIBB,
MAURICE GIBB and ROBIN GIBB

Moderately slow, with a beat

preach - er talked with me and he smiled,_____ said, The
I told him I'm in no hur - ry, but if
laughed but that did - n't hurt,_____ and it's

"Come and walk with me, come and walk one more mile._____ Now for
I broke her heart, then won't you tell her I'm sor - ry. And for
on - ly her love that keeps me wear - ing this dirt._____ Now I'm

IT'S MY PARTY

Words and Music by HERB WIENER,
WALLY GOLD and JOHN GLUCK, JR.

Moderately bright

No - bod - y knows___ where my John - ny has gone,___ But
Play all my rec - ords, keep danc - ing all night,___ But
Ju - dy and John - ny just walked thru the door,___

Ju - dy left___ the same time.
leave me a - lone___ for a - while,
Like a queen___ with her king,

Why was he
'Til John - ny's
Oh, what a

LAND OF A THOUSAND DANCES

Words and Music by CHRIS KENNER
and ANTOINE DOMINO

82

LET'S LIVE FOR TODAY

Words and Music by GUIDO CENCIARELLI,
GIULIO RAPETTI and NORMAN DAVID SHAPIRO

LOUIE, LOUIE

Words and Music by RICHARD BERRY

MAGIC CARPET RIDE

Words and Music by RUSHTON MOREVE
and JOHN KAY

MCA music publishing

MONDAY, MONDAY

Words and Music by
JOHN PHILLIPS

MY BOYFRIEND'S BACK

Moderately

Words and Music by ROBERT (BOB) FELDMAN,
GERALD (JERRY) GOLDSTEIN and RICHARD GOTTEHRER

My boy-friend's back, and you're gon-na be in trou-ble.
He's been gone for such a long time.

(Hey, la - di - la, My boy-friend's back)

When you see him com-in', bet - ter
Now he's back and

(Hey, la - di - la, My boy-friend's back)

cut on the dou-ble.
things will be fine.

You're

MR. CUSTER

By FRED DARIAN,
AL DeLORY and JOE VanWINKLE

Moderately

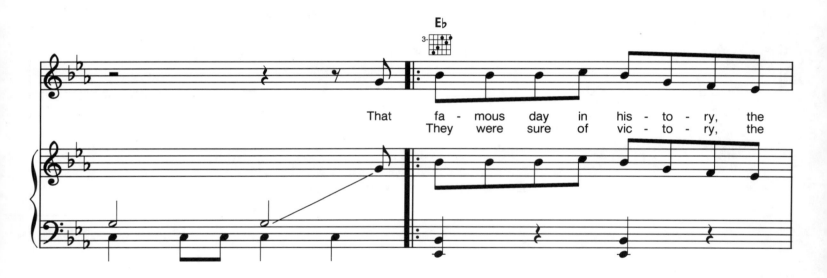

That fa - mous day in his - to - ry, the
They were sure of vic - to - ry, the

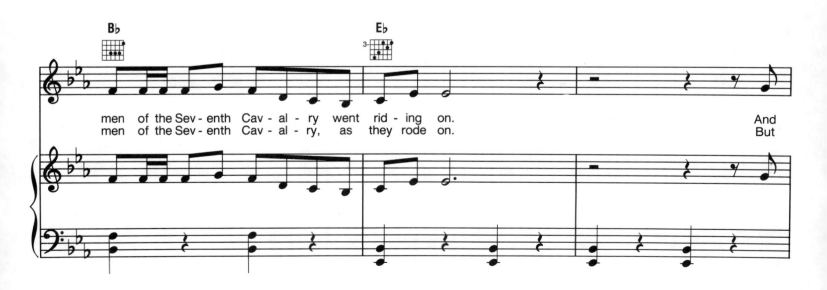

men of the Sev - enth Cav - al - ry went rid - ing on.
men of the Sev - enth Cav - al - ry, as they rode on.

And
But

103

Please don't make me go.
Please don't make me go.

There's a

I had a dream last night about the com - ing
red - skin a - wait - ing out there. He's fix - ing to take my

fight.
hair.

Some - bod - y yelled "at - tack" and
A cow - ard I'm be - ing called 'cause

G7

then I don't wan-na stood with an ar-row in my back.
I stood wind up dead___ or___ bald.

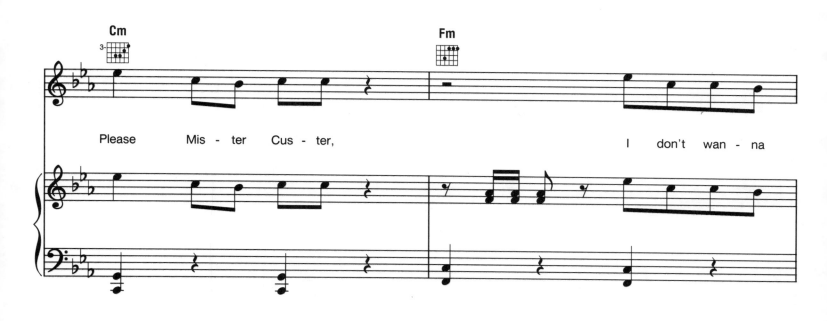

Cm   **Fm**

Please Mis - ter Cus - ter,   I don't wan - na

Cm

go.   No!   (Spoken): Look at
(Spoken): I wonder what

RUNAROUND SUE

Words and Music by
DION DI MUCCI and ERNIE MARESCA

110

NA NA HEY HEY KISS HIM GOODBYE

Words and Music by GARY DeCARLO,
PAUL LEKA and DALE FRASHUER

PEOPLE GOT TO BE FREE

Words and Music by FELIX CAVALIERE
and EDWARD BRIGATI, JR.

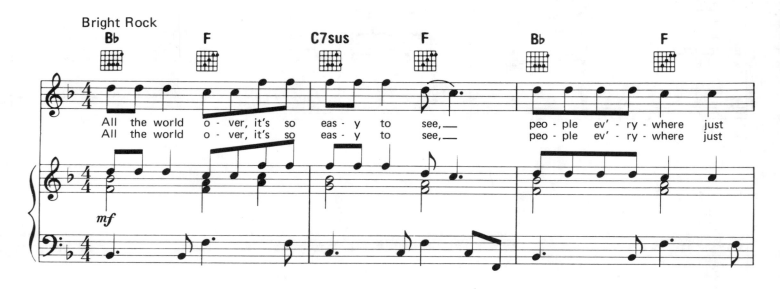

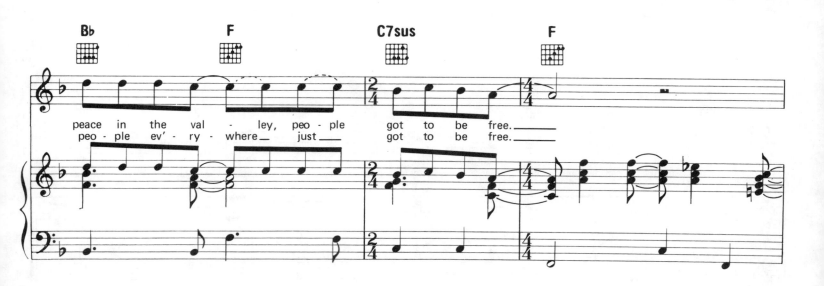

116

RUNNING BEAR

Words and Music by
J.P. RICHARDSON

Moderately

On the bank of the ri - ver stood Run-ning Bear, young In - dian
swim the rag - ing ri - ver 'cause the ri - ver was too
Bear dove in the wa - ter lit - tle White Dove did the

brave. On the oth - er side of the ri - ver stood his
wide. He could -n't reach lit - tle White Dove wait - ing
same. And they swam out to each oth - er through the

love - ly In - dian maid. Lit - tle White Dove was a
on the oth - er side. In the moon - light he could
swirl - ing stream they came. As their hands touched and their

RUNAWAY

Words and Music by DEL SHANNON
and MAX CROOK

Moderately Bright

THE SHOOP SHOOP SONG
(IT'S IN HIS KISS)

Words and Music by
RUDY CLARK

124

SAVE THE LAST DANCE FOR ME

Words and Music by DOC POMUS
and MORT SHUMAN

SOUTH STREET

Words and Music by KAL MANN
and DAVE APPELL

STAND BY ME

Words and Music by BEN E. KING,
JERRY LIEBER and MIKE STOLLER

134

SPINNING WHEEL

Words and Music by
DAVID CLAYTON THOMAS

STAY

Words and Music by
MAURICE WILLIAMS

SUGAR SHACK

Words and Music by KEITH McCORMACK
and FAYE VOSS

SUMMER IN THE CITY

Moderately, with a steady beat

Words and Music by JOHN SEBASTIAN,
STEVE BOONE and MARK SEBASTIAN

145

sum-mer____ in the cit-y.____

sum-mer____ in the cit-y.____

(Instrumental)

D.S. and Fade
(Instrumental)

THE SUNSHINE OF YOUR LOVE

Words and Music by JACK BRUCE,
PETE BROWN and ERIC CLAPTON

Well, it's get-ting near dawn ___
I'm with you my love, ___

when lights close their tired ___ eyes.
the light shin-ing through ___ on ___ you. ___

149

THE TWIST

Words and Music by
HANK BALLARD

TOBACCO ROAD

Moderately with a back beat

Words and Music by JOHN D. LOUDERMILK

Grew up in ___ a rust - y shack ___ All I had was
Bring dy - na - mite and a crane ___ Blow it up was start all

hang - in' on my back, On - ly you ___ know how I loathe ___
ov - er a - gain Build a town ___ be proud to show ___

This place called To - bac - co Road ___ but it's home
Give the name ___ To - bac - co Road ___ but it's home

The on - ly life I've ev - er

156

UNDER THE BOARDWALK

Words and Music by ARTIE RESNICK
and KENNY YOUNG

Oh, when the sun beats down ___ and burns the
park you hear ___ the hap - py

tar up - on the roof, ___ And your
sound of a car - ou - sel, ___ You can

shoes get so hot you wish your tired feet ___ were fire -
al - most taste the hot - dogs and french - fries ___

THE WANDERER

Words and Music by
ERNEST MARESCA

Oh well,

I'm the type of guy ____ that would nev-er set-tle down, ____ where
Flo on my left arm ____ there's _ Mar-y on my right, ____ and
I'm the type of guy ____ that ____ likes to roam a-round, _ I'm

pret-ty girls are, ____ well, you know that I'm a-round; ____ I
Jan-ie is the girl ____ that I'm dat-ing to-night; ____ And
nev-er in one place, _ I ____ go from town to town, ____ And

WHITE ROOM

Words and Music by JACK BRUCE
and PETE BROWN

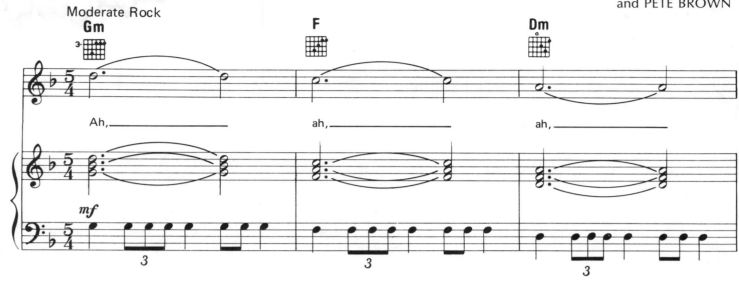

Moderate Rock

Ah,_____ ah,_____ ah,_____

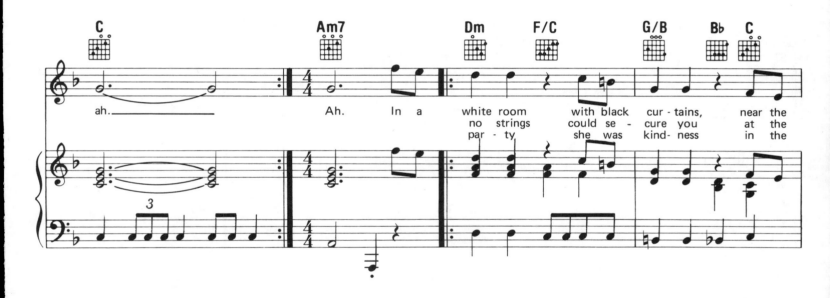

ah._____ Ah. In a white room with black cur - tains, near the
no strings could se - cure you at the
par - ty she was kind - ness in the

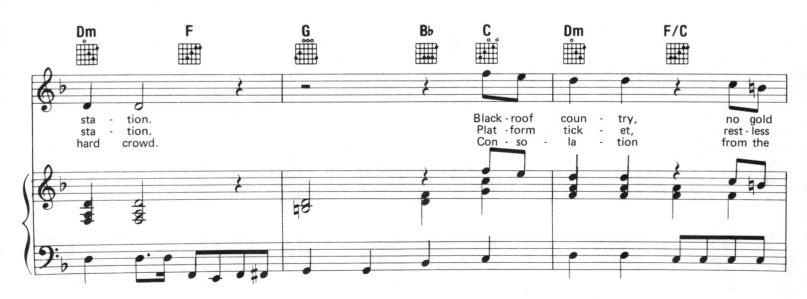

sta - tion.
sta - tion.
hard crowd.

Black - roof coun - try, no gold
Plat - form tick - et, rest - less
Con - so - la - tion from the

164

A WHITER SHADE OF PALE

Words and Music by KEITH REID
and GARY BROOKER

WILD THING

Words and Music by
CHIP TAYLOR

WOOLY BULLY

Words and Music by
DOMINGO SAMUDIO

1. Mat-ty told Hat-ty
2,3. *See additional lyrics*

A-bout a thing she saw.

Had two big horns

Bul - ly____

Additional Lyrics

2. Hatty told Matty
   Let's don't take no chance,
   Let's not be L 7
   Come and learn to dance
   Wooly bully — wooly bully —
   Wooly bully — wooly bully — wooly bully.

3 Matty told Hatty
   That's the thing to do,
   Get yo' someone really
   To pull the wool with you —
   Wooly bully — wooly bully
   Wooly bully — wooly bully — wooly bully.

Rock on!

With more Great Music Books From Hal Leonard Publishing

THE BEST OF 80'S ROCK

33 hot chart songs from the decade, featuring: Centerfold • Don't You (Forget About Me) • Every Breath You Take • Heart And Soul • Hold Me Now • I Love Rock 'n' Roll • It's Still Rock and Roll To Me • Pour Some Sugar On Me • Pride (In The Name Of Love) • Round And Round • Sweet Dreams (Are Made Of This) • Walk This Way • What's Love Got To Do With It • You Give Love A Bad Name. **Arranged for Piano, Voice and Guitar.**
00490215 ....$12.95

BEST ROCK SONGS EVER

70 of the best rock songs from yesterday and today, including: All Day And All Of The Night • All Shook Up • Ballroom Blitz • Bennie And The Jets • Blue Suede Shoes • Born To Be Wild • Boys Are Back In Town • Every Breath You Take • Faith • Free Bird • Hey, Jude • I Still Haven't Found What I'm Looking For • Livin' On A Prayer • Lola • Louie, Louie • Maggie May • Money • (She's) Some Kind Of Wonderful • Takin' Care Of Business • Walk This Way • We Didn't Start The Fire • We Got The Beat • Wild Thing • more! **Arranged for Piano, Voice and Guitar.**
00490424 ....$14.95

CONTEMPORARY — THE ULTIMATE SERIES

75 recent hit songs, including: Can't Smile Without You • Careless Whisper • Could I Have This Dance • Could've Been • Don't Worry, Be Happy • Endless Love • Eternal Flame • Every Breath You Take • Every Rose Has Its Thorn • Fast Car • Girl I'm Gonna Miss You • Good Thing • Holding Back The Years • I Write The Songs • I'll Be Loving You (Forever) • Imagine • Islands In The Stream • Man In The Mirror • Memory • One More Try • Sara • She's Like The Wind • Somewhere Out There • Through The Years • We Didn't Start The Fire • What's Love Got To Do With It • With Or Without You • You Needed Me. **Arranged for Piano, Voice and Guitar.**
00490289 ....$16.95

THE DEFINITIVE ROCK 'N' ROLL COLLECTION

A classic collection of the best songs from the early rock 'n' roll years — 1955-1966. 96 songs, including: Barbara Ann • Chantilly Lace • Dream Lover • Duke Of Earl • Earth Angel • Great Balls Of Fire • Louie, Louie • Rock Around The Clock • Ruby Baby • Runaway • (Seven Little Girls) Sitting In The Back Seat • Stay • Surfin' U.S.A. • Wild Thing • Woolly Bully • and more. **Arranged for Piano, Voice and Guitar.**
00490195 ....$19.95

METAL ROCK HITS

A hot collection of 20 hard rock hits, including: Bad Medicine • Free Bird • Love Bites • Purple Haze • Walk This Way • Livin' On A Prayer • Round And Round. **Arranged for Piano, Voice and Guitar.**
00360482 ....$10.95

ROCK ON!

A collection of 50 top rock hits spanning the decades from the 60's to the present. Includes such rock classics as Free Bird • A Whiter Shade Of Pale • Sunshine Of Your Love • Maggie May • more. **Arranged for Piano, Voice and Guitar.**
00360932 ....$12.95

For more information, see your local music dealer, or write to:

Hal Leonard Publishing Corporation

P.O. Box 13819 Milwaukee, Wisconsin 53213

Prices and availability subject to change without notice.